GW00340785

THE BIRDS OF

LEEDS CASTLE

Leeds Castle
Maidstone, Kent
ME17 1PL
Tel +44 (0) 1622 765400
Fax +44 (0) 1622 735616

email enquiries@leeds-castle.co.uk
www.leeds-castle.co.uk

© Leeds Castle Enterprises Ltd. 2001

CONTENTS

5   INTRODUCTION

6   HISTORY

8   THE AVIARY TODAY

     – CONSERVATION IN ACTION

10   ABOUT BIRDS – DESIGN AND ADAPTATION

14   FEATHERS

16   EYES AND EARS

18   FOOT FUNCTION

20   NUTRITION AND DIET

22   BEHIND THE SCENES

     – INCUBATION AND REARING ROOMS

24   BIRD HOSPITAL

contents

26 SOFTBILLS

28 HORNBILLS

30 PARAKEETS AND COCKATOOS

32 LORIES AND LORIKEETS

34 MACAWS

36 AMAZON PARROTS

38 SPOONBILLS, IBIS AND THICK-KNEES

40 THE DUCKERY

42 WATERFOWL AT LEEDS CASTLE

44 BLACK SWANS AT LEEDS CASTLE

46 WILD BIRDS OF LEEDS CASTLE

48 BIBLIOGRAPHY, ACKNOWLEDGMENTS AND MAP

THE AVIARY
AT LEEDS CASTLE
IN OCTOBER 1992

INTRODUCTION

Olive, Lady Baillie, the last private owner of Leeds Castle, died in 1974. She bequeathed a place of outstanding beauty and tranquillity to the Leeds Castle Foundation. Beyond the walls of Leeds Castle itself she created a haven for bird life, both native and exotic. Across the estate can be seen Kingfishers, Green Woodpeckers, Great Crested Grebes, Mute Swans, Tufted Ducks and many more species including Goosanders on their annual winter visits.

Gouldian Finch

Lady Baillie introduced onto the Castle Moat some of the first known Black Swans in the country in the 1930s. We now have a resident population of eight breeding pairs who roam freely over the grounds.

In the early 1960s a breeding environment for both exotic and native waterfowl was created by Stéphane Boudin and Russell Page, interior designer and garden designer respectively, in an enchanting spot between the main entrance to the grounds and the Wood Garden. This pond with its surroundings is known as The Duckery.

In the early 1950s the first Australian finches were kept on the castle island. These were housed in a small lean-to aviary built onto the side of the Maiden's Tower. This was the beginning of what was considered at the time to be the best collection of exotic birds in the country, specialising in the beautiful pastel-coloured Australian Parakeets, Cockatoos and the Indian Blue Ringneck Parakeet. Although Australian species are still represented in our Aviaries, we have diversified the collection which now houses over 100 species from around the world. Parrots, softbills and wading birds can all be seen here, many being part of international captive breeding programmes.

HISTORY

During her convalescence from an incapacitating leg injury Olive, Lady Baillie began to indulge what was to become her passion. Her time of recuperation allowed her to develop her interest in birds, particularly Australian species.

The collection, which started with a few Australian Finches and a small number of Black Swans, soon expanded to become a significant part of the Leeds Castle estate.

140 aviaries were designed, and constructed along the bank next to the river Len (before the creation of the Great Water in 1982), where the Lady Baillie Garden now is.

Black Swan drinking.

The care and management of this growing collection demanded the attention of someone as enthusiastic and devoted as Lady Baillie herself. In 1953 Peter Taylor, a gardener on the estate, was formally employed as Lady Baillie's birdman. This was a partnership that was to continue until Lady Baillie's death in 1974 and created one of the most prestigious collections of birds in Europe. Lady Baillie's collection was one of the first to successfully breed rare Australian Parakeets such as the Brown's Rosella, the Hooded Parakeet, the Pileated Parakeet and many species of Lory and

LADY BAILLIE'S BIRDMAN, PETER TAYLOR at the opening of the new Aviary in 1988, accompanied by two young friends and a Blue and Gold Macaw, a species from Central and South America.

Lorikeet. It was however their successes with the rare Indian Blue Ringneck and other naturally occurring colour mutations that remain the chief memory for many people visiting Leeds Castle today. The Yellow Ringneck Parakeet can still be seen here at Leeds and still breeds successfully. Peter Taylor continued his work with Lady Baillie's collection until his retirement in 1993.

Indian Blue Ringneck
Parakeet

Yellow Ringneck
Parakeet

7

THE AVIARY TODAY
CONSERVATION IN ACTION

On the 25th May 1988, the new Aviary bearing Lady Baillie's name at its entrance, was opened by our Royal Patron, HRH Princess Alexandra. This Aviary was designed by the architect Vernon Gibberd of London, who incorporated the most progressive ideas and the advice of leading aviculturalists.

It was also in the late 1980s that a new emphasis emerged within the bird-keeping community: the need to establish self-sustaining captive populations. These days, the number of different species has been decreased in order to allow room for more pairs of some of the more threatened species.

Queen of Bavaria Conure

An endangered species, due to the loss of habitat in its native South America.

The design of the new Aviary moves away from the traditional rows of square enclosures and aims to provide specific habitats for each group of birds housed. All our birds have suitable mates, nesting facilities, protection from adverse weather conditions, the best quality diets and a territory which is safe and secure.

Toco Toucan

chick successfully parent reared in 1992.

It is the creation of such appropriate, stress free and closely-monitored environments that make captive breeding programmes so successful. With a number of species now on the verge of extinction, great co-operative efforts are being made world-wide to breed and reintroduce captive bred young of endangered species into their original habitats. Young birds raised here go to other responsible breeding projects with similar aims, so making a significant contribution to avian conservation. We are also proud to have received to date three UK First Breeding Awards. These awards are for the Von der Decken Hornbill (*Tockus deckeni*) in 1990; the Fischers Touraco (*Tauraco fischeri*) in 1992 and, in 1997 the Crowned Hornbill (*Tockus alboterminatus*).

Australian King Parrot

The Male Australian King Parrot has striking plumage whereas its female counterpart is relatively dull. This is an example of sexual dimorphism.

ABOUT BIRDS
DESIGN AND ADAPTATION

A bird is an advanced aerodynamic achievement of natural selection, specialised in complex ways to varying modes of existence - 8,900 of them, to be precise, that being the number of known species today. Parrots, Parakeets, Lories and Macaws make up 339 species - within which there are many subspecies.

Chestnut
Breasted
Finches

Black Cockatoo

A rare Black Cockatoo from the Cape York Peninsula, New Guinea and the islands of Australasia.

Birds have an extremely rapid metabolism requiring high-quality food. They are very warm-blooded, their average temperature being between 140°F and 170°F. However, once acclimatised, they have no problems with a colder climate than that found in their natural habitat (here feathers play a crucial role). The English weather is therefore no bar to tropical species being kept in normal climatic conditions.

Strong wings and heart, flexible feathers, and minimum body-weight make the miracle of flight possible. Bones are hollow, and any joints not essential to flight are fused together to decrease overall weight. Weight is further limited in the female by the fact that she lays eggs instead of carrying young. There are extensive airsacs throughout the body.

The East African Crowned Crane is one of two Crane species at Leeds Castle Aviary; with its smaller Eastern European cousin, the Demoiselle Crane.

Opposite: One of Leeds Castle's resident Whooper Swans, being fed by two young visitors.

African Spoonbill

The appropriately named Spoonbill uses its remarkable bill to sift through water and mud to extract its food of crustaceans.

In addition to the famous Black Swans, Leeds Castle has rare Black-Necked Swans (above), from South America and the Falkland Islands, and resident Whooper Swans (left), normally winter visitors to the UK from Scandinavia and Siberia.

Birds' bones are unique in the animal kingdom, being filled not with marrow, like those of mammals, but with air cells.
The weight they bear is minimal, enabling strong support of the well-developed flight muscles.

Wings of aircraft were designed using birds' wings as a model. The distance from the leading edge of the wing to the trailing edge is greater on the upper surface than it is on the lower. As air flows over the upper wing surface it must travel faster than air over the lower surface, thus creating a vacuum on the upper surface. It is this vacuum that actually lifts the bird into the air. This is called an aerofoil. By varying the angle of the wing in relation to the oncoming air, speed of flight can be controlled.

The European Spoonbill - a close relative of its African counterpart - as seen in the aviary, breeds in Holland and several individuals make the short journey across the North Sea to visit the Eastern Counties of the UK during the summer months. Possibly due to climate change and suitable wetland habitats, it is thought that one or two pairs are now breeding in secret locations.

Shelduck

The Shelduck breeds in this country and is to be found on estuaries and in marshy areas. In recent years there has been a decline in their numbers, possibly due to pressures on their habitat.

Ringed Teal

Hawaiian Ne-Ne Goose

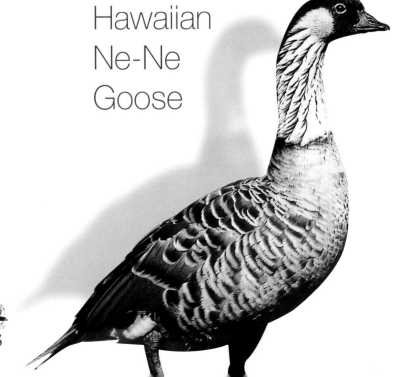

FEATHERS

By ruffling its feathers a bird can contain an envelope of heat around its body, and by sleeking them it allows heat to escape (a bird has no sweat glands); a constant body temperature is thus maintained.

Green
Winged Macaw

feathers

THERE ARE THREE TYPES OF FEATHER EACH WITH ITS OWN APPEARANCE AND SERVING A SPECIFIC FUNCTION:

CONTOUR FEATHERS

These form the outer surface of the bird and serve to give the bird its shape, colour and streamlining. They overlap rather like roof tiles.

FLIGHT FEATHERS

These may be long or short depending on the type of environment the bird inhabits. For example, birds from open areas which sometimes soar, will have longer flight feathers than a forest bird which only requires short bursts of speed.

DOWN FEATHERS

These loose-formed feathers are held close to the body, under the contour feathers. Some birds such as those which come from a cold or wet environment may have many of these feathers to keep them warm – the best known example being an Eider Duck whose down feathers are used to make eiderdowns.

A House Sparrow for example, has about 2,000 feathers, while a Swan may have up to 22,000. Once a feather has been formed, it is a dead horny structure. After a year a bird's feathers are usually well-worn and are all replaced in the annual moult.

Feathers, which are thought to have evolved from reptilian scales, provide insulation besides facilitating flight. With birds as with human beings temperature variations in a short space of time can cause illness. Heat loss however does occur through the un-feathered areas of facial skin, beak and feet – that is why a bird will sleep standing with one leg folded into its body and beak tucked under its wing.

The male Peacock's long tail has two functions; balance and display. To attract a mate and to ward off other suitors, the Peacock fans its tail to produce a remarkable spectacle of a hundred shimmering 'eyes'.

In common with the Peacock, the male Mandarin Duck has equally flamboyant plumage, designed for the intricacies of ritualised courtship. Interestingly, both these species were introduced to Europe from the Far East; the Mandarin Duck from China, and the Peacock from Java and Malaysia.

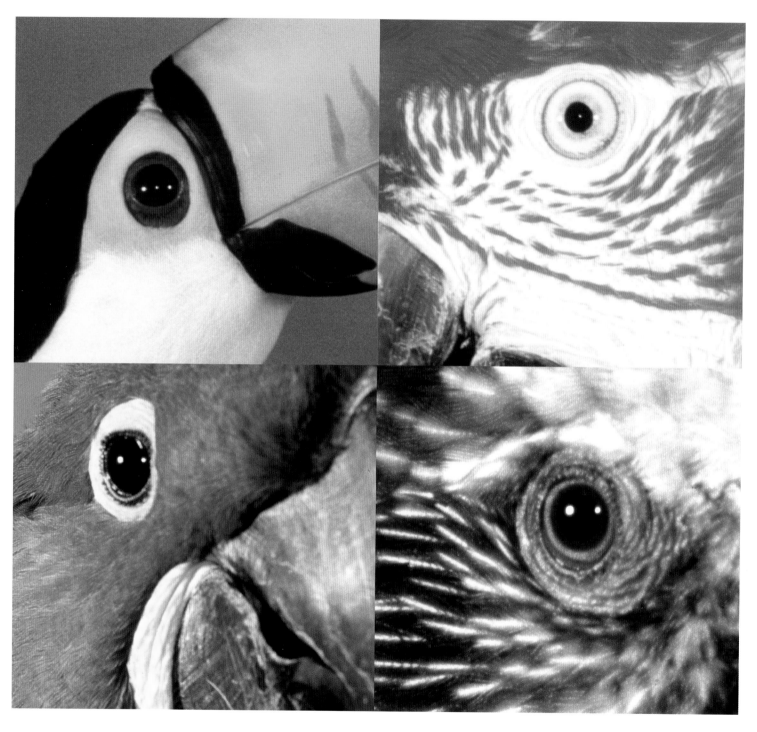

EYES AND EARS

Birds gather all the information needed for survival through their eyes and ears. A bird's eyes are more powerful than any other animal's, and very large in comparison to the head, allowing more room for the motion sensors, and giving the bird a much larger and sharper image than is the case with the human eye. This type of vision is essential to a fast-moving animal. Some birds including Parrots have binocular vision, that is a sharper image over a wider area and this together with the placing of the eyes on the side of the head, enables vision in all directions with little head movement – highly useful in bird of prey species.

Bali Starling

The rarest Starling in the world, there are only 26 birds surviving in the wild. At Leeds Castle the species is part of an internationally managed captive breeding programme.

Birds make many different sounds and respond to them in numerous ways. It is not that birds hear *better* than man, they simply hear so much *more*. They can distinguish tones or frequencies lying very close together. Their songs and calls communicate to other birds and contain rapid sequences at milli-second intervals that the human ear cannot follow.

Kea

The Kea is a resident of the mountains of the South Island of New Zealand. Although an endangered species due to the pressures on its habitat, it is numerous within its range. These highly adaptable and intelligent birds have learnt to benefit from human contact, and investigate all sources of food, often causing havoc to property and vehicles. In the breeding season, they are to be found upwards of 600 metres above sea level, where they make their nests in a crevice under rocks, or among the roots of a tree.

FOOT FUNCTION

Most birds have four toes on each foot; three pointing forward, one backwards. These are used for perching, walking, hopping, eating and killing.

Of the world's 8,900 species of birds, 5,000 are known as passerines or perching birds.

Moluccan Cockatoo

When a bird perches, its toes lock around the branch. Tendons passing down the back of the leg to the toes are automatically pulled taut over the ankle bone, so that the toes curl in. As long as it is in the squatting position, its toes stay clamped around the perch. They unlock only when it stands upright, releasing the tension on the tendons.

ADAPTATIONS

Wading birds have long legs for use in water eg. Herons, Flamingoes, Avocets, or for walking in long grass eg. Cranes and Storks.

Walking birds such as pheasants have a reduced hind toe, so keeping the minimum area of foot in contact with the ground.

Running birds are often flightless and long-legged, such as Ostriches and Rheas. They have only two toes similar to fast running mammals, where the toes are reduced from five to two, for example deer and antelope, or even to one in the case of the horse.

SPECIALISTS:

SWIMMING - webbed feet
eg: Ducks

CATCHING AND HOLDING - talons on birds of prey
eg. Hawks and Owls

CLIMBING - two toes forward and two toes back
eg. Parrots and Woodpeckers

Leeds Castle Aviary has been highly successful in breeding this striking wading bird. Since World War II, the Avocet has increased in numbers in this country, primarily due to the efforts of the RSPB (Royal Society for the Protection of Birds), and the bird breeds on many reserves on the East coast of England, notably Titchwell in Norfolk and Minsmere and Havergate Island in Suffolk.

Waders such as Avocets are specially adapted to the environment in which they live. Their long legs enable them to feed at a greater depth of water than many other species. Their beaks are long, slender and slightly upturned, enabling them to effectively skim insects and other invertebrates off the surface of the water. This specialisation, however, makes them vulnerable to changes to their environment.

NUTRITION AND DIET

A variety of wild birds feed at the edge of the Moat: Coot, Jackdaws, Mallard Ducks and a Canada Goose.

All birds require foods rich in energy and cell-building materials. The digestive system of different species has developed in accordance with their different feeding habits. The tree-feeding Amazon Parrots have a natural high-fibre diet for example, while the ground-feeding Australian Parakeets and Cockatoos eat a variety of seeds.

At the Leeds Castle Aviary, diets are formulated after careful examination of each species' feeding habits in the wild, and wholesome and fresh foodstuffs are combined to approximate to species' specific preferences. The amount of food provided is such as to induce the birds to consume proper proportions of a well-balanced diet. Leeds Castle also contributes to research into the nutrition of species where little is known about the actual composition of foods consumed in the wild, for instance the Toco Toucan which is remarkably efficient at absorbing iron from its diet.

A Bali Starling being offered a locust at the Leeds Castle Aviary.

Seeds, nuts and vegetables form the complex nutrition necessary for Parrots.

The endangered Kea thrives at the Aviary on
a mixed diet of fruits, vegetables and seeds.

BEHIND THE SCENES –
INCUBATION
AND REARING ROOMS

 One of the main objectives of the Aviary is to breed the species within its care. Most of our birds have successfully reared their own chicks and are excellent parents. Sometimes however problems arise either through the inexperience of a new parent or an over-zealous male. In these instances, either eggs or chicks are at risk and may need to be removed for artificial incubation and hand-rearing.

It is very difficult to duplicate with complete accuracy the natural incubation of a hen bird, especially during the first few days of incubation. The egg must be brought up to temperature slowly and the degree of weight lost must be controlled by providing the correct humidity. The first stages of development inside the egg are critical, as this is when the internal organs are formed.

There are four important factors that must be controlled to guarantee good success when hatching an egg artificially: humidity, temperature, turning and ventilation.

The avian egg starts developing after it has been fertilised, even before it has been laid by the hen. As the egg passes down the oviduct, the egg white is being deposited on the already developing embryo which is attached to the yolk sac. This development stops when the egg is laid and the temperature drops. The embryo lies dormant during this time and if necessary can be stored for up to ten days.

Candled egg
Egg illumination showing the development of the embryo

Development resumes when the egg is brought back up to incubation temperature, usually 37.5 degrees C. but will die if the temperature drops a second time.

During the time the egg is waiting to be laid, what is to become the embryo has already grown into several thousand cells. During the first few days of incubation, many complex developments are progressing within the egg. By about the fourth day most of the organs have begun to appear and about a week later the embryo looks like a bird.

During the remainder of the time until hatching, the chick's various organs grow and develop, preparing it for "popping" out of the egg. Before leaving the egg, the yolk sac withdraws into the body where it will serve as nutrition during the first few days after hatching.

Once successfully hatched and dried, the chick is then moved into a brooder where the temperature and humidity are carefully regulated. After approximately 8 - 12 hours the chick will be ready for its first feed and the time-consuming duty of hand-rearing begins. Depending on the species being reared, the chick may be on a meat, seed, or fruit-based diet and this is carefully worked out well before the chick hatches. Feeds may be as frequent as every two hours day and night, depending on the protein content of the diet and the body weight of the chick being reared.

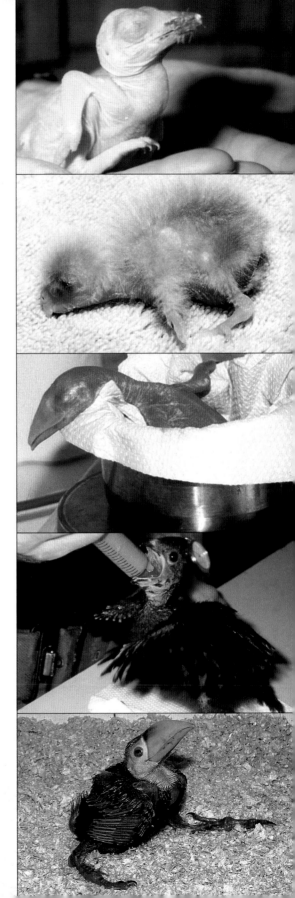

Newly hatched Kookaburra chick.

Newly hatched Parakeet chick covered in fluffy down feathers for extra warmth.

Toco Toucan chick at 3 days old, weighing 113gms.

Young White-Cheeked Touraco chicks are born with their eyes open and a thick black down.

Toucan chick at 5 weeks of age.

Bird Hospital

Our Bird Hospital is designed to provide our birds with all the care they would need in any emergency or illness. It is very important to isolate an ill bird from the others, to ensure that the other birds do not become infected. Birds recovering from a physical injury need isolation to recuperate without trauma from people or other birds.

It is extremely important for our keepers to pay close attention to their birds, learning the different postures that indicate any change from the normal. The change in behaviour may be very slight, such as holding the feathers fluffed, reduced activity, reduction or rapid increase in food consumption, or a dull appearance to the eyes. A bird that looks a little '*off colour*' may be very ill, so obviously

something is done immediately to determine the cause. In order to protect themselves from predators, birds have developed the ability to hide an illness or injury. Birds of the same or similar species may drive a sick bird from their territory and food supply. This will force the bird to seek new foraging areas where it is not familiar with the food sources or possible dangers.

Leeds Castle uses the services of The International Zoo Veterinary Group which is made up of veterinarians specialising in different areas of animal medicine and whose services are utilised all over the world by the foremost zoological institutions. Our Bird Hospital is fully-equipped to help us to deal with every basic emergency until the veterinarian arrives.

Young Blue-Fronted Amazon Parrots learning to eat solid food.

Entrance to the Aviary

The brightly-coloured Hoopoe inhabits gardens, orchards and agricultural land, and uses its long slender bill to pick out larvae and insects from the earth and from beneath the bark of trees. Widespread throughout the Continent, the European Hoopoe is a regular and colourful Summer visitor to Southern and Eastern England. The smaller Asian Hoopoe breeds sucessfully at Leeds Castle.

SOFTBILLS

The term 'Softbill' encompasses a wide diversity of species. The name is a reflection of their diet, which comprises varying combinations of fruit, insects and nectar depending on the species.

Softbills range from the Toco Toucan with its lightweight but massive beak, designed to reach the choicest fruit - its main diet is found on the very tips of branches - to the tiny Hummingbirds, whose beak and tongue have adapted to sip nectar from flowers.

In line with the Leeds Castle policy of providing its birds with the very best in nutrition, locusts and mealworms are fed to the Softbills all year round.

Asian
Hoopoe

Violaceous touraco

Toco Toucan

HORNBILLS

Hornbills derive their name from the brightly-coloured beak with decorative casque which is so typical a feature of these birds. The species represented in Leeds Castle Aviary are found in Africa, and nest in tree holes.

The male incarcerates the female in the nest by building a mud wall over the nest hole. He then feeds the female through a small slit left in the wall. When the young are fully developed and feathered, the hen breaks out of the nest to join her mate and the young rebuild the wall with the nest debris, sealing themselves in again.

The Hornbill's long slit-shaped beak is perfectly adapted to passing food through the narrow entrance to the nest. This nesting behaviour ensures the chicks are safe from predators during the rearing process. The chicks leave the nest soon after the hen, but continue to beg for food for one month after fledging.

Leeds Castle is proud to have been awarded the UK First Breeding for both species of Hornbill housed within the Aviary: the Von der Decken Hornbill in 1990 and the Crowned Hornbill in 1997.

Von der Decken's Hornbill

PARAKEETS AND COCKATOOS

One-sixth of the world's species of Parrots and Parakeets, of the greatest diversity and beauty, are found in Australia. Lady Baillie was particularly fond of birds from this area, and when her collection of Australian birds was first established in 1958 it was the most complete and well presented in the UK. The soft pastel colours of the Parakeets and Rosellas are a wonder of nature.

Cockatoos are among the most intelligent members of the Parrot class. These birds are easily recognisable by their crest, which is raised when a bird is excited or alarmed; they love to bathe in a Spring shower, and will hang upside down by their feet, allowing the water to run down between their feathers.

As well as being highly intelligent, the Cockatoos form deep emotional bonds with their mates and therefore should only be kept in pairs; Cockatoos do not make ideal pets. Neither would you want to argue with that strong beak; the name Cockatoo is derived from a Malay word that means 'pincer'.

Splendid Grass Parakeet

Black Cockatoo

Leadbeater, or
Major Mitchell's
Cockatoo

Goldies
Lorikeet

LORIES AND LORIKEETS

This unique family of birds is distributed throughout South-eastern Asia, Papua New Guinea, Australia and Polynesia. These birds have a specially adapted tongue with a brush-like tip, enabling them to collect pollen and nectar from flowers. The birds at Leeds Castle are provided with a specially prepared nectar from the Diet Kitchen. These birds are also very fond of fruit and buds. As a result of their feeding habits, Lories and Lorikeets play a major role in the pollination of trees and flowering plants in the wild.

Lories and Lorikeets are arguably among the most beautiful of the world's birds, some also ranking among the most intelligent and charismatic with an insatiable desire to cause mischief.

Goldies Lorikeet

Stella's Lorikeet

This is the 'melanistic', or black form of the
Red Stella. Leeds Castle's pair of melanistic Stellas
have produced both black and red chicks.

Scarlet Macaw

Military Macaw

An endangered species.

The Hyacinth Macaw

is the largest of the Macaw family
and an endangered species.

Macaws

 Macaws are found in South and Central America. Most species belong to the genus *Ara*, and are characterised by a large facial area of naked skin which will flush pink when a bird is excited.

All Macaws possess a long tail which distinguishes them from other Amazon parrots. These birds have distinct personalities, a strong social structure, and super intelligence and, like the cockatoo, should be kept in pairs.

Amazon Parrots

Most species of Amazon Parrots climb about in the tree tops in forested areas foraging for food in flocks of up to 30 or more birds, two or three species often feeding together. These birds don't spend much time flying, but they will move to large communal roosts at night, when as many as 1,500 birds may be present. This flocking behaviour is thought to be a method of defence as the birds could be vulnerable to predators whilst feeding and sleeping.

During the breeding season, Amazon Parrots become particularly territorial, and a pair will defend their nest site in a hollow tree with vigour. The Patagonian Conure is however, a highly gregarious species and remains social throughout the nesting season. These birds dig deep nesting burrows in limestone or sandstone cliff sites. The birds at Leeds Castle have been bred successfully using an artficial nesting cliff.

Yellow-Nape Amazon

Patagonian Conure

Hawk-Headed
Parrot

African Spoonbills

Scarlet Ibis

Sacred Ibis

SPOONBILLS, IBIS AND THICK-KNEES

Peruvian Thick-Knee

Alongside the Aviary's main collection of Parrots, Softbills and Passerines, are a variety of long-legged birds of interest. The Scarlet Ibis is a resident of the Everglades in Florida and the Sacred Ibis is to be found along the Nile and throughout Africa. In common with the Spoonbill, to which they are related, they use their long bills to find food deep down in mud and sand.

The Peruvian Thick-Knee's long legs have evolved for running at speed across the sandy scrubland it inhabits in South America. The Thick-Knee is a close relative of the Stone Curlew which breeds in Southern and Eastern England on the Brecklands, and on chalky heaths and agricultural land.

An aerial view of Leeds Castle, showing the Duckery in the foreground, the Cedar Pond and beyond, the Moat.

THE DUCKERY
- A RECOLLECTION

 In the early 1950s the area now comprising the Duckery was a wilderness of fallen trees, brambles and nettles, with a few mature standards, largely oak. The lake was silted up to the extent that the water only just flowed along one side, and alders grew thickly on either bank. The cascade was almost hidden by undergrowth. In about 1955 it was decided to clear the area simply to give some impression of care and cultivation because since the end of World War II, the Wood Garden and Park had slowly been brought back under control and this area was noticeable for its air of neglect.

The alders were felled, the rubbish was dragged up into heaps and burnt, the lake was dredged and the silt pulled out on to the flat area now bisected by the long path. The next stage was to cultivate the area covered with the highly fertile silt from the lake, largely to combat the enormous growth of unusual weeds that always result from this type of operation. Once this was done, three very large oval beds of *rhododendron ponticum* were planted roughly equidistant down the length of the site. Grass was sown between and kept roughly mown. This lay-out persisted until the advent of the waterfowl around the mid-1960s. The erection of the rodent-proof fence was the first essential, and this was quickly followed by a 'landscaping

scheme, devised by Stéphane Boudin and Russell Page. The three main features of this were: removal of the rhododendron beds, the introduction of the Chinese bridge and the building of the *'Pavillon des Canards'*. The latter has a significance of its own because its exact positioning was so highly indicative of the way two great designers anticipated the aesthetic pleasure of their client. The pavilion with its sheltered seat was sited exactly so that one looked up over the cascade and saw a part of three historic ages of Leeds: The Maidens Tower, the New Castle and the southern fringe of the Gloriette, framed by cedar trees. Alas, the 'frame' has succumbed to gales.

Shrubs were introduced along the bank of the stream parallel to the lake and large quantities of daffodils were placed on the far banks of the stream to be seen from the Duckery. On the further side, nearer the front drive, there was less organised cultivation so as to provide breeding cover for the waterfowl.

The waterfowl themselves all began from eleven birds owned by a Mrs Weston in Warwickshire. She advertised in *Cage Birds* for *'a perfect home'* for the remnants of her collection, as she was forced by circumstances to abandon her home. The allure of such a *'crie de coeur'* was irresistible to another bird lover – *'Female Chestnut-Breasted Teal. Find it a mate at once!'*. From these humble beginnings, with the usual enthusiasm, drive, initiative and attention to detail of the

Hooded Merganser

This striking species of waterfowl is a member of the Sawbill family, and originates from North America. Sawbills have a series of sharp teeth used to grip their prey of small fish which they catch by making deep dives.

collector, sprang a considerable collection of waterfowl. Not for her the 'individual pen system' of Slimbridge, quite correct for their purposes, but at Leeds it was to be 'togetherness and happiness'. Some mistakes were made in the initial stages as to which varieties should be included. Eventually however a comprehensive, individually docketed wing-tabbed collection appeared. It was loved and nurtured by its owner.

Each winter the resident wildfowl population of the Duckery is swelled by an influx of other ducks and geese.

WATERFOWL AT LEEDS CASTLE

The origins of the waterfowl population at Leeds Castle go back to the Thirties, when Lady Baillie kept some of the earliest known Black Swans in the country. As mentioned in the previous 'recollection' it was in the early Sixties that a breeding environment for the waterfowl was created by Stéphane Boudin and Russell Page, in what was a virtually derelict area of the estate. This now enchanting spot between the main entrance and the wood garden became known as the Duckery.

This area with the fast flowing cascade of water and the wide pond make an ideal environment for a variety of ducks and geese. Lady Baillie enjoyed watching the birds from the small summer house situated at the beginning of the Chinese bridge. For hours she would watch nesting birds and was amused by their habit of trying to disguise their nest location by walking past it many times before returning to their eggs.

Over the years a collection plan has been compiled which lists the species able to thrive in these conditions and live happily on a colony basis. Species kept by Lady Baillie included Black Necked Swans, Eider Ducks, Red Breasted Geese and Barrow's Goldeneye. Except for the latter all can still be seen at Leeds Castle today. Species that regularly breed here include the rare and formerly critically endangered Hawaiian Ne Ne Goose, the Red Breasted Goose - also an endangered species, the Ross' Snow Goose and the Barnacle Goose. Duck species breeding in the Duckery include Pintail, Shoveler Mandarin and Carolina, Red Crested Pochard and Hooded Merganser. A greater number of European ducks and geese are now kept so that the birds may breed freely and boost the wild populations.

Clockwise from left:
Whooper Swans, Red-Breasted Geese, Hawaiian Ne Ne Geese,
North American Ruddy Duck and Barnacle Geese.

waterfowl

Ross Snow Geese

43

BLACK SWANS AT LEEDS CASTLE

Before World War II, Lady Baillie had some of the earliest known Black Swans in the country. However, at the end of the war there were no birds at Leeds. It was in the early 1950s that Lady Baillie managed to obtain a pair of these birds from her cousin, the late Mr. Whitney Straight, who had managed to maintain a small stock of the swans throughout the war. Since then Black Swans have been kept here continuously with occasional exchanges with other collections such as Slimbridge, in order to keep the population healthy. These elegant and regal birds have become an emblem for Leeds Castle and now number eight breeding pairs which roam freely over the estate.

WILD BIRDS OF LEEDS CASTLE

Whatever time of the year, a visit to Leeds Castle provides excellent birding opportunities, near the castle itself and around the grounds. In winter the moat is host to unusual waterfowl, such as the GOOSANDER - a member of the Sawbill family - and the Duckery's resident population of wildfowl is swelled by a variety of wild ducks and geese.

The moat's reedbeds provide nesting sites for GREAT CRESTED GREBES and Reed and Sedge Warblers, and with many areas of water within the grounds, all three species of Wagtails are regularly seen. The spectacular KINGFISHER can be seen mainly during summer, darting across the moat in the area of the gatehouse, barbican and fortified mill.

CORMORANT

The woods hold Blackcap and the commonly seen Willow Warbler and several pairs of SPOTTED FLYCATCHERS nest in and around the castle buildings and the Culpeper Garden area. Both the Great Spotted Woodpecker and the GREEN WOODPECKER are resident here, but the Green Woodpecker is most often heard rather than seen, with its distinctive laughing call. Even without binoculars, larger birds such as the Heron and the Cormorant are not difficult to see.

The more common raptors (birds of prey), such as the Kestrel and the increasingly numerous Sparrowhawk, are regularly seen in the grounds, and the HOBBY, a striking breeding visitor to southern England, has been sighted occasionally in the summer.

BIBLIOGRAPHY

The Aviary at Leeds Castle by D Frank
Philip Wilson Publishers 1988

Practical Incubation by Rob Harvey
Published by Rob Harvey 1990

Lories and Lorikeets by Rosemary Low
Paul Elek Ltd. 1977

*A Complete Checklist of the Birds
of the World* by Howard and Moore
Academic Press 1994

USEFUL ADDRESSES

The Avicultural Society
c/o Bristol Zoological Gardens,
Clifton, Bristol BS8 3HA

The Parrot Society
108b Fenlake Road,
Bedford MK42 OEU

The Association of British Wild Animal Keepers
c/o Leeds Castle, Maidstone,
Kent ME17 IPL

The British Waterfowl Association
c/o M. Griffiths, Beech Lodge,
Ide Hill, Sevenoaks, Kent TN14 6BB

The Royal Society for the Protection of Birds (RSPB)
UK Headquarters,
The Lodge, Sandy, Bedfordshire SG19 2DL

ACKNOWLEDGEMENTS

Thanks to Dave Frank for allowing me to use material from his previous guidebook, and also to John Brook whose knowledge about the wildlife on the Leeds Castle estate has been invaluable.

Particular thanks to Peter Taylor who has given me access to Lady Baillie's collection of birds through his own recollections and breeding records. I should also like to thank him for all his years of dedication to Lady Baillie's birds. Without Peter there would probably not be an Aviary at Leeds Castle today.

Laura Gardner, Curator of Leeds Castle Aviary, December 2000.

Text by Laura Gardner.
Designed by Nick McCann.
The photographs in this book are primarily by David Hosking, Nick McCann and Peter Smith. Additional photographs are by Barry Duffield, David Frank, Stuart Thomas and Richard Ward. Photographs on pages 46 and 47 are by courtesy of RSPB Images: Goosander and Spotted Flycatcher - Steve Knell, Kingfisher - Michael W Richards, Green Woodpecker - Mark Hamblin, and the Hobby - Carlos Sanchez Alonso.

Produced and published for Leeds Castle Enterprises Ltd. by Heritage House Group Ltd. Heritage House, Lodge Lane, Derby DE1 3HE Tel: +44 (0) 1332 347087 Fax: +44 (0) 1332 290688 email: publications@hhgroup.co.uk
Printed in Great Britain © Leeds Castle Enterprises Ltd. 2001